MW01000057

My Chicken Soup for the Soul™

Personal Journal

Health Communications, Inc.
Deerfield Beach, Florida

©1996 Jack Canfield and Mark Victor Hansen
ISBN 1-55874-484-3 (hardcover)

Publisher: Health Communications, Inc.
           3201 S.W. 15th Street
           Deerfield Beach, FL 33442-8190

Cover Design by Andrea Perrine Brower
Text Illustration by Larissa Corinne Hise

*"...Sit back, relax and enjoy the powerful journey
you are about to begin ..."*

"You are about to embark on a wonderful journey."

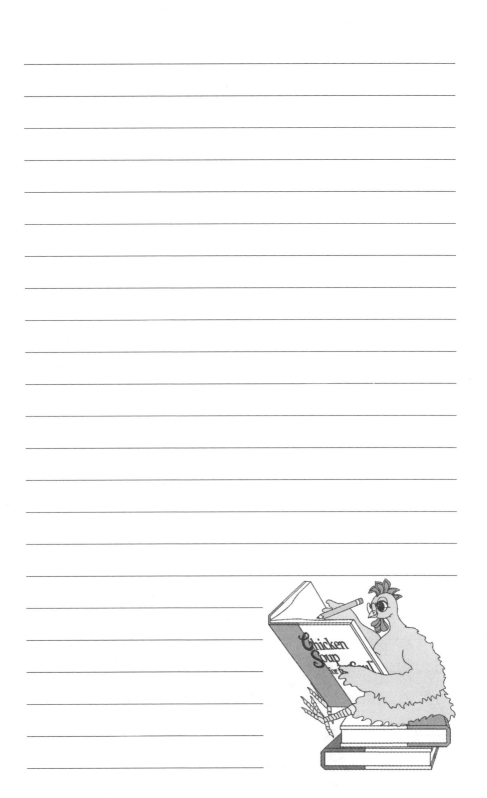

"...Stories are one of the most potent ways to transform our lives. They speak directly to the subconscious. They lay down blueprints for living."

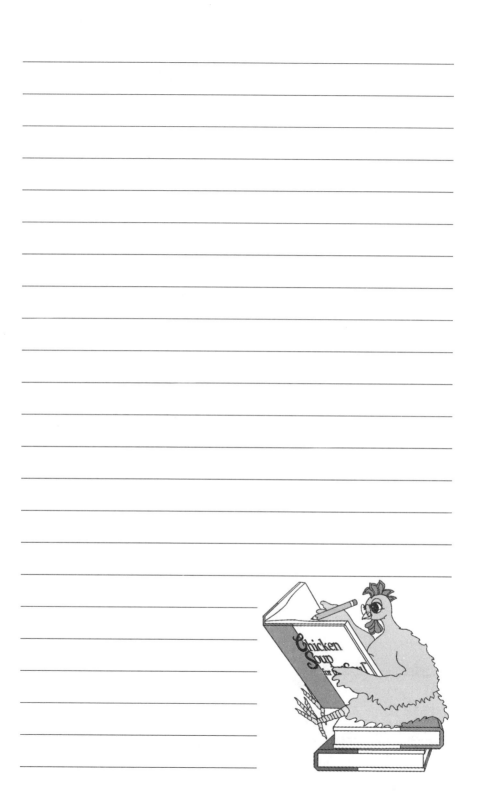

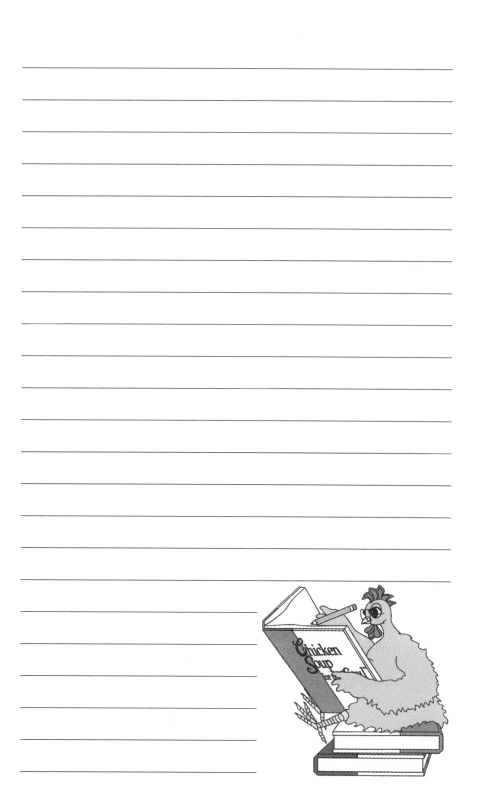

_____

_____

.
_____

_____

_____

_____

_____

_____

_____

_____

_____

_____

_____

_____

_____

_____

_____

_____

_____

_____

_____

_____

*"Stories are powerful vehicles that release our energies
to heal, to integrate, to express and to grow."*

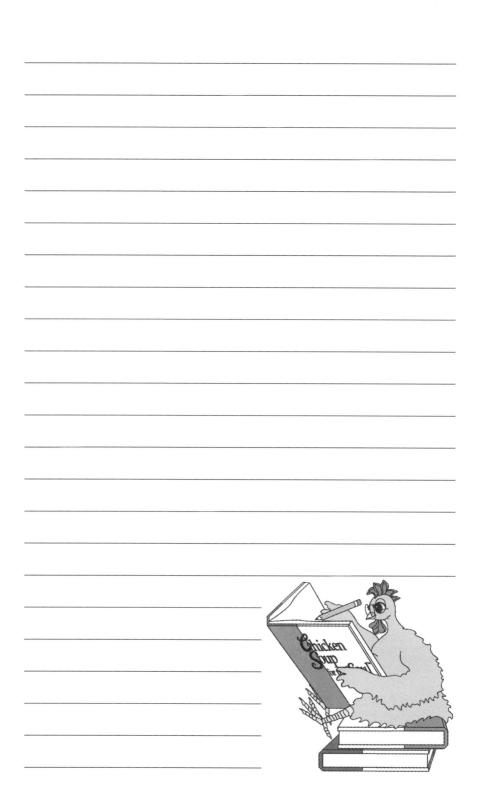

_____

_____

_____

_____

_____

_____

_____

_____

_____

_____

_____

_____

_____

_____

_____

_____

_____

_____

_____

_____

_____

_____

_____

_____

_____

*"Don't hurry through this book. Take your time. Enjoy it.
Savor it. Engage it with your whole being."*

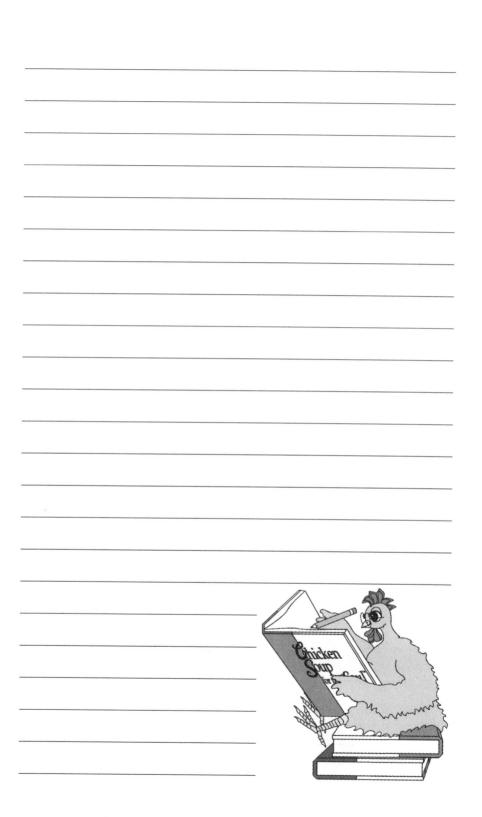

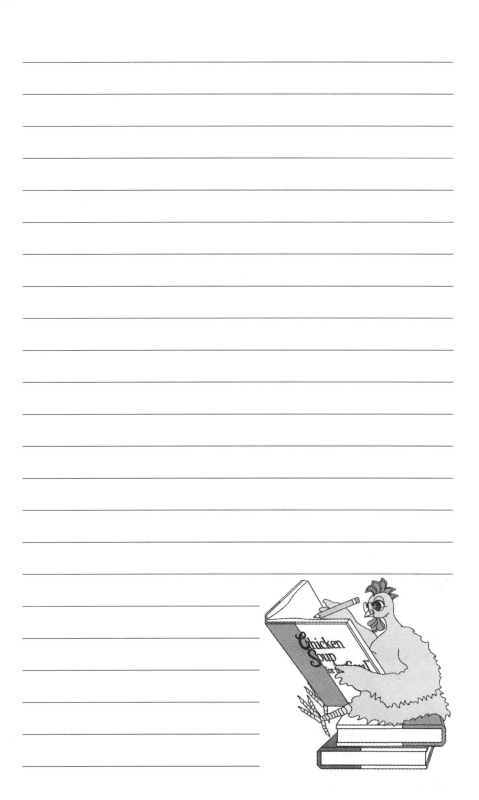

_____

_____

_____

_____

_____

_____

_____

_____

_____

_____

_____

_____

_____

_____

_____

_____

_____

_____

_____

_____

_____

_____

*"Slow down. Listen to the words in your heart as
well as your mind."*

*"Savor each story. Let it touch you. Ask yourself,
what does it awaken in me?"*

"Let yourself have a personal relationship with each story."

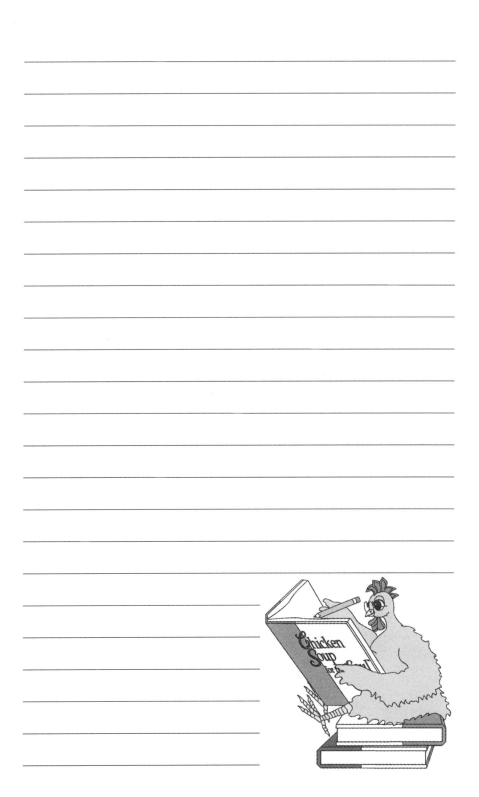

"People may need to hear your story."

"...You have your hands on a book that will warm the heart, awaken the soul, and rekindle the spirit."